The Passive Income Blueprint
Drop Shipping Edition:

Create Passive Income with Ecommerce
using Shopify, Amazon FBA, Affiliate
Marketing, Retail
Arbitrage, eBay and Social Media

By

Income Mastery

ii

Table of Contents

Before we begin I have a free gift for you from Russell Brunson - for those of you that don't know Russell Brunson is, he's the man that created Click Funnels. In my opinion it's the best funnel website out there and it has also helped create the most millionaires. Any form of passive income you are going to build, you will 100% need to leverage funnels of some sort. If you're reading this book, then you want to be the best in your industry. This book will give you the play by play to have people PAYING you for your advice. I am able to give you his best selling book for free right down here. I only have a few copies left so please get them while you can. Just click this http://bit.ly/giftfunnelbook

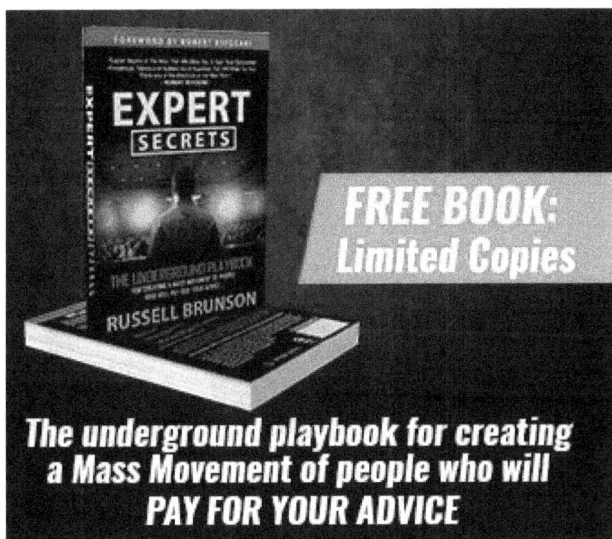

Introduction

Online commerce is booming, and it has never been a better time to get involved with dropshipping. If you're looking for an entrepreneurial endeavor that has low-startup costs and incredible potential for growth, then read on! Dropshipping has become one of the most steadfast ways to build an online business and the best part is that you do everything electronically! You don't need to spend a fortune on building up a stock, you don't need to physically handle products to ship and you certainly don't need to rent a storefront. All you need is a computer, a passion for business and a plan!

This book will cover everything that you need to know about dropshipping, from the basics of setting up your own business, to avoiding the common pitfalls of such an endeavor. We'll be going through each step of the process, explaining what dropshipping is, how it all works and most importantly, how you can make money off of it. If you've heard successful entrepreneurs talk about dropshipping before and want to know how it can benefit you, then read on!

Chapter 1: What is Dropshipping?

Dropshipping is the practice of selling an inventory without handling the physical products yourself. Thanks to the power of online connectivity, you don't need to purchase products in bulk and then store them if you want to sell them! Instead, you work to create a dropshipping system, where you source your goods from a manufacturer or wholesaler, create an online store and then work with the supplier to fulfill orders.

Dropshipping is a purely online business, allowing for you to acquire and sell products through your own online storefront. Thanks to websites like Shopify, who have plugins that can aid in the process of dropshipping, you can run a fully functioning sales store all from the comfort of your own home. More than that, you can expedite and automate processes, freeing up your time to focus on your entrepreneurial goals.

In order to understand the dropshipping process, you need to consider how products are sold and distributed. A supplier has goods in storage, but they don't sell their goods to customers directly. Rather, they rely on a middleman, known as a retailer to purchase the goods at a wholesale price. The retailer then marks up the goods and sells them on the market.

A dropshipper is someone who gets involved in the final step of the sales process. Rather than produce or handle the goods themselves, they simply market and sell products on their website. When a product is purchased, the dropshipper takes the order and sends it to the supplier, who then packages the product up and sends it on its way to your customer.

In a way, a dropshipper is similar to traditional retailer, with the major exception that they never touch the products in the sales process. This means that they don't have to spend money on stock or costly storage fees. Instead, their main focus is creating an online storefront, where they create brands sell products to customers.

Dropshipping is a great online business for those who don't have a large amount of capital to start a traditional business. With the low barrier to entry and the ease of learning, you could get your own business going within a few weeks of starting.

Better yet, there are plenty of people out there who have been able to quit their jobs and focus on dropshipping full time!

But to achieve that level of success takes time and most importantly, an understanding of the ins and outs of dropshipping. If you've always wanted to run your own business but have struggled with the costs, then you might want to give dropshipping a try. It's not hard to do and more importantly, you will learn plenty of important lessons about entrepreneurship and responsibility.

The costs are low, the work is rewarding and there is plenty of potential for growth and sales. If all of that sounds like a good idea to you, let's move on to the next chapter and examine the benefits of dropshipping in comparison to other business models.

Chapter 2: Pros of the Dropshipping Model

Dropshipping itself has many pros and cons. Within this chapter, we'll cover the primary positives of the dropshipping model.

Dropshipping requires very little capital investment

One of the biggest drawbacks to running a traditional brick and mortar store is the fact that it is quite costly to do so. You must have a large amount of capital to get started, so that you can acquire things such as property, supplies, etc. However, dropshipping's model requires a much smaller amount of capital for starting up.

The biggest costs you'll face at the beginning will be website acquisition and tools to assist you with finding niches, all of which are minimal when compared to the regular price points of starting a business. If you have a shoestring budget, you can certainly start dropshipping!

It's Super Easy to Get Started

There are no real barriers to entry when it comes to dropshipping. All you need is time and dedication to go through the necessary steps to find a supplier, build an online storefront and do the necessary research for the types of products you want to sell. You don't have to get a license, go through courses or spend a fortune on some kind of beginner's toolkit to get started. In fact, you could get started as soon as you finish this book.

There's less overhead costs

Traditional stores have a high level of overhead. Things such as rent, paying to keep the lights on and staff wages can all cut into the profit of the business. However, with dropshipping, you won't have to worry about these types of overhead costs. You won't have to operate a physical storefront, nor will you have to maintain your own inventory. Instead, you'll simply have to pay for things like web hosting and credit card services, all of which are significantly cheaper than a month's rent of physical space!

Access to a wide selection of products

The types of products that you can sell are virtually unlimited. As long as you are able to find a supplier who can meet the demand and is willing to work with you, you can sell any product you like. And you don't have to specialize in just one type of product, either. You can work with as many suppliers as you like, yet sell all your products on one storefront. As long as you are able to handle the logistics of working with each supplier independently, there is no limitation to what you can offer in your store!

It's not difficult to scale

Once you've gotten the hang of how to run a dropshipping operation, you'll find that scaling your business upwards isn't that hard to do. Higher amounts of orders can actually be cheaper, as it often translates into bulk discounts from suppliers. Whether you're selling 100 products a month or 1,000 a month, the principles of dropshipping remain the same. All that really changes is the profit margins!

Access to a global market

One of the most valuable components of dropshipping is the fact that you're operating entirely online. This gives people from all over the world access to your shop. As long as you are able to offer decent international shipping rates, you will be able to attract customers from anywhere on the planet. This widens your market significantly more than if you were running a physical storefront.

It can be easily automated

Dropshipping does require a fair amount of work, but the good news is that there is a large portion of that work that you can automate. There are quite a few apps and services out there that offer smart services that can help with some of the more time-consuming tasks. From automatically creating and printing shipping labels, to keeping track of inventory, these automation tasks will save you hundreds of hours of time.

There's no shortage of suppliers and manufacturers

One of the most important tasks when it comes to dropshipping is finding suppliers and manufacturers who would be willing to work with you. Once located and negotiated with, these suppliers will provide you with the products necessary to sell online. Thanks to the connectivity of the internet and the ability to work with anyone, anywhere, you will find that there are no shortages of suppliers and manufacturers. As long as you are able to show them that you have a business plan put together and have a legitimate sales platform, you should have no trouble convincing them to provide you with products to sell!

Ultimately, drop shipping allows for you to bypass many of the traditional roadblocks that stand in the way of starting a business. The ability to connect to the global market, save money on overhead and scale the business as you grow in ability and customer base make dropshipping one of the most attractive online business models out there. However, this isn't to say that dropshipping itself has no drawbacks. Let's move on to the next chapter, where we'll look at the cons of dropshipping.

Chapter 3: Cons of the Dropshipping Model

It's important to be aware of the drawbacks and shortcomings of any business model before you get involved. This chapter will highlight some of the challenges, problems and frustrations that can come with the dropshipping model. This shouldn't discourage you from getting involved, rather it is meant to help you accurately understand some of the challenges that you will face as you get more involved in this business.

Sudden Stock Shortages

Resources in this world are not unlimited. There will be times where for some reason, a supplier is unable to meet demand for a product. Either, demand has swelled up so much that the products are moving off the shelves too quickly, or some logistical problems have interfered with creation of the product. Regardless of the reason, there can be situations in which you have a bunch of orders and not enough products to ship out. This will require quick adaptation and work on your part to figure out how to fulfill those orders, either by finding another supplier quickly, or by delaying shipping, which can create customer service issues.

Higher cost of goods sold

Prices can shift due to a variety of economic and market factors. Something might be selling cheaply today, but tomorrow, the prices can go up. If that's the case you'll either have to find a cheaper selling solution or eat the cost yourself, which can cut into margins. Prices don't always fluctuate, but it is a possibility when working with suppliers and manufacturers.

Higher fulfillment costs

Fulfillment can be one of the more expensive parts of the business. Shipping rates, handling and service fees can all eat into your margins. You'll have to be vigilant in finding ways to reduce these costs as much as possible, but as more and more people get involved with dropshipping, some suppliers find that they now have the luxury of charging more for services.

More customer service issues

Since you don't have a hand in the packaging and shipping process, there are bound to be errors that will happen. A customer may end up receiving a product that is damaged or has not been properly packaged. Sometimes they may end up getting the wrong order. Fulfillment facilities tend to process a lot of orders and not everything can be done perfectly each time. You can expect that there will be mishaps that happen over time.

You don't have full control over the business

Being a dropshipper is being a middleman. You are creating a storefront and displaying products, but in reality you don't have any physical access to those products. At the end of the day, there are going to be things that are out of your hands. While you can work as hard as you can to ensure that there won't be inventory issues, that product quality stays high and that people get orders fulfilled in a timely manner, all of that is left in the hands of other people. You can only react and adapt accordingly to the situations and problems as they come up, but your ability to prevent these types of problems are limited due to lack of full control.

Reliance on Inventory

Without inventory, you don't have a business. Finding good suppliers who are reliable and able to provide you with the inventory that you need is crucial. Since you don't own the products yourself and you don't have them stored up in your own warehouse, you'll need to work to ensure that you have an adequate inventory at all times. If a supplier cannot meet demand suddenly, you'll find yourself in a world of financial hurt.

Potential Quality Control issues

Since you aren't directly working with the products, that means standards for quality can slip over time. You will need to closely monitor your products, testing them every now and then to ensure that they are staying at the same quality levels that you are promising your customer. The last thing you want is for a large shipment of mediocre or low-level quality products to be released. But, since you aren't directly responsible for the production or shipping of those products, you will have to trust the supplier or manufacturer to steadily keep the quality as high as possible.

Overcrowded markets

The lost cost to get started, combined with the fact that anyone with decent business sense can run a dropshipping operation means that the markets can be quite overcrowded. You will have to deal with competition and fight to find some way to distinguish your own business from others. This can be remedied somewhat by finding the right kind of niche for your product, but with new dropshipping websites opening up every day, you will eventually have to deal with some form of competition.

No guarantee of profits

Like all business endeavors, there is simply no guarantee that you will see profits from a dropshipping operation. Of course, the only people who guarantee profits are the ones who are trying to profit off of you! The fact is, dropshipping has risks in it. The good news is that with such a low cost of entry, you won't have to risk tens of thousands on an idea. But you should still no that there is no guarantee that you will see a return on your investment, just like any entrepreneurial endeavor.

Requires *Basic* technical skill

Dropshipping does require that you have some basic technical skills. You'll need to know how to operate a computer, how apps work, as well as how to market and negotiate. The first two skills aren't hard to learn, but many people balk at the idea of marketing and negotiation. Still, those two skills are necessary if you want to find any level of success in your dropshipping operation.

More products or suppliers means more work

Using multiple suppliers greatly increases the complexity of your operation. You will have to track multiple companies, remember each supplier's rules and procedures, as well as maintain quality control checks from different sources. This can prove to be a bit overwhelming, especially if you are inexperienced. However, you can use automation services to help reduce this complexity, but there are still challenges associated with increasing the size of your supplier or product pool.

Low margins

In the dropshipping business world, your margins aren't going to be crazy high. The reason behind this is that the accessibility of the business type means that there will always be competition, and competition keeps pricing low. The easy entry into the market means that margins will always stay rather low, since you don't need to invest a large amount of capital to get started. So if you're expecting to make a large amount of profit in a short amount of time, you will be disappointed with dropshipping. There is plenty of money to be made, but it takes time to establish a business that is able to generate a larger amount of profit.

Shipping complexities

Shipping, you will find, is one of the more complicated issues in the dropshipping world. There are a lot of things that can go wrong in the time it takes for a customer to click the buy button and for the package to arrive at their house safely. You will have to create a method of effectively providing suppliers with shipping information that is both accurate and quick. You'll face delays sometimes, as well as problems caused by the shipping companies themselves, such as losing your packages. This is all part of the process, but it can cause frustration in customers.

Overall, the perils of dropshipping really come from the fact that you aren't in direct control of the production and distribution of your products. Then again, these two factors are also the main benefit behind dropshipping, as you don't have to pay to produce and store items on your own.

Over time, you will find that these unique challenges can be overcome by proper planning, by forethought and quick thinking when problems rear their ugly heads. You don't have to be intimidated by this list, but you should ask yourself if these are the types of things that you can handle. Dropshipping is an active type of business, you will have to regularly work at building it up. If you're looking for a passive way to generate income, be warned that there is quite a bit of work involved with dropshipping. The good news is that once you get in the groove of things and have some experience under your belt, you will find that the business can be both fun and profitable!

Chapter 4: Starting Your Own Dropshipping Business

Before You Begin

Before you get started with following all of the instructions within this book to set up your own dropship business, you'll need to really consider if this is the right business for you. Dropshipping takes time, energy and effort. It is not a simple get-rich quick scheme and it certainly isn't something that you can set up and then leave to run on its own accord. You will have to actively manage this business, spend time learning the ins and outs and more importantly, be constantly working to improve the operational side of the business.

Dropshipping is an investment of time and money. The more that you are willing to invest, the more returns that you will see. This is not a business for the faint of heart, it is a growing, changing affair that constantly shifts over time. There is tremendous potential for financial gain, as long as you are willing to put in the work.

So, if you're looking for a project that has potential to increase your wealth and are willing to put in the time to get what you want, then go for it! But if you aren't ready to give 100% to the business, if you aren't willing to spend hours upon hours of study and preparation, then you might want to consider a different business idea. There are plenty of other, more casual types of businesses out there, but dropshipping is only for those who are ready to seriously invest themselves. Anything less than full focus and attention will result in minimal returns.

The Mindset Required to Succeed

Success in business can be tough to achieve. Making money isn't an easy task, if it were, then everyone would be doing it. But the truth of the matter is that financial success with dropshipping requires grit and hustle. Things will not go well for you in the beginning. There will be plenty of failures, accidents and missteps that can threaten your business. You will be faced with making mistakes that every beginner makes. You may end up losing a bit of money in the process.

Grit is the ability to endure these hardships and keep pressing forward. True grit allows for you to push on and stick to your plan, regardless of how tough things can get. Running a business is hard, much harder than simply just showing up for work at some other job. When you're an employee, you don't have to stomach risk and tough decisions. At the end of the day, you get paid for what you're doing, regardless of how much money the company makes. But being a business owner is fundamentally different.

When you're the owner, everything is on you. How much money you make is determined by your hustle, by your energy level and most importantly, by your business decisions. You don't have anyone to fall back on when you're the one calling the shots. Yet at the same time, this also means that you are the one who gets the lion's share of the profits. You are ultimately responsible for the success or failure of your business, and that responsibility comes with a higher paycheck, as long as you can tough it out.

The mindset of success is simple: endure the problems that present themselves to you and hustle every day. Work as much as you can to make money, increase your number of clients and create a strong brand and you will find that your business will grow and thrive. Take it easy, slack off or wait for opportunities to show up and your business will dwindle down.

If you want to succeed, you need to embrace full responsibility. In the end, your business is 100% yours, to do with as you please. You can be successful, but it will take time. Treat each failure or mistake as an opportunity to learn and don't give up due to frustration with where you currently are. Real success is the ability to stick out failure, learn from your mistakes and then press forward. Don't be too hard on yourself. At the end of the day, as long as you are willing to keep working at it, you will find success in the dropshipping business!

Educate Yourself

There are a lot of options when it comes to getting started with dropshipping. Sometimes you can be overwhelmed by the sheer number of choices that you will have to make at the beginning. The best place to start is simply through research. Spend a large chunk of your time reading about dropshipping, studying how to properly do it, look at case studies and read other success stories. The more that you soak in about dropshipping, the clearer the future will look to you.

Education is your primary weapon when it comes to being successful in this field. While hard work is necessary to get a product off the ground, education and research will provide you with the right directions. It doesn't matter how fast you can sprint, if you're going in the wrong direction you'll only end up lost. So start out with an intense regimen of study and research. You should know all of the ins and outs of dropshipping before you actually get started. That way, as you go along, you'll only need to return to educational material as a reference point.

Create a Business Plan

Once you've spent the time to learn everything about dropshipping, it will finally be time to get started on building a functional business plan. The business plan will contain everything about your dropshipping operation. It will cover what you are selling, how you plan to obtain access to those products, your branding and marketing ideas, as well as your goals for the operation.

A fully written out plan is necessary for giving you focus. By creating palatable goals and listing out the steps that you will take to achieve them, you will be able to focus on checking off that list each day. You won't have to wonder "what's next?" because you will have planned everything in advanced. In addition to that, having a good business plan is invaluable when working with suppliers. Most suppliers want to know that they are working with legitimate professionals, not a person with fly-by night ambitions.

You'll need to list out things like your niche, target demographic, a list of suppliers that you will contact, which platform you intend to sell on as well as what automation systems you will be using. We will be covering all of these throughout the course of this book.

Financing Your Dropshipping Business

Dropshipping can be done rather cheaply, so you don't have to worry too much about raising capital. The best strategy for financing your business is to simply use money that you've saved. Sure, you'll risk losing that money, but you won't have to worry about paying back any kind of loan or other investors. Then, as you make a profit, you can reinvest that money directly into the dropshipping business, expanding your potential for more profit. This is the safest and healthiest way to finance your business.

Determination, passion and education are necessary if you want to succeed in the world of dropshipping. As long as you are able to focus on putting in the hours and learning the tricks of the trade, you will be able to make money with dropshipping. Over the next few chapters, we'll be digging into the specifics of the dropshipping process, starting with the supply chain and ending with handling inventories. There is a lot of information to take in, so go at your own pace, learn as much as you can and once you feel ready, start working on a business plan. There's no reason to rush. As the adage goes, measure twice, cut once. You don't want to waste your time and money by just running into dropshipping headfirst. You have all the time in the world to build a great, effective business.

Chapter 5: Understanding the Supply Chain and Fulfillment Process

In order to be able to understand your role as a dropshipper, you'll need to understand how the supply chain works. There is a long, complicated process that happens in between buying a product and then receiving it, usually involving multiple groups of people who all play a very specific role. These roles determine the chain of distribution, beginning with production.

Manufacturers

A manufacturer is just that, a company that physically creates the products that will end up sold in stores. Manufacturer's can be as small as a one-man operation, creating artisan soaps out of his home, or it can be as be as large as a major factory, mass producing cell-phone covers. Manufacturer's vary in both sizes and in policy. A manufacturer will create the product and then sell to wholesalers or retailers, which are then sold for a markup. It is rare to see a manufacturer willing to directly sell to the general public, as they often prefer to make their money through sales to wholesalers.

Manufacturer's often required minimum purchase orders in order to obtain their supplies. Thus, in order to be able to work directly with a manufacturer, you must be able to provide them with a minimum number of purchase orders. These minimums are often quite large, so for most dropshippers who are starting out, they will need to work with a wholesaler instead.

Wholesaler

A wholesaler is the one who purchases the products made by manufacturers. They make large purchase orders, buying in bulk and then in turn, sell their products to retailers for a markup. This is where they make their profit, as the mark-up is usually much higher than the cost of acquisition. A wholesaler's business model is usually centered around acquiring products and then selling to retailers, instead of focusing on selling to the public.

Retailer

A retailer is a company or individual who purchases a product from a wholesaler and then sells that product for a higher markup. As a dropshipper, you are considered to be a retailer, although the specifics are a little different, as you aren't paying for the product until after you've already sold it. Traditional retailers place orders to wholesalers, pay for the stock and then sell it in their storefronts. A dropshipper only places the purchase order when they have made a sale, relying on the wholesaler to fulfill the shipping and handling.

Consumers

The consumers are the people who make the decision to purchase products. Consumers don't actually care to know the specifics of where a product comes from. Their perception is generally that the retailer that they are buying from is the one responsible for the product. Discussion of wholesalers or manufacturers doesn't matter to them, as those two suppliers are not directly involved with the sale. The only thing that matters to a consumer is the retailer in front of them. Most consumers won't ever know that you are a dropshipper, because they don't care to know. Products and good customer service experiences are the things that drive their purchasing decisions.

The Dropshipping Process in Action

When looking at the four groups above, it is easy to see how they all fall into a cycle. The manufacturer creates, the wholesaler buys, the retailer sells and the consumer purchases the end product. The dropshipper has the ability to get involved with any of the three types of supplier. You might be able to convince a manufacturer to fulfill orders for you, or you could work with a wholesaler to set up a dropshipping fulfillment system, so you can directly sell their stock on your own websites. You could even work with a retailer, if they are willing to fulfill on your behalf. It doesn't matter how a dropshipper gets stock, what matters is that the dropshipper is the one who makes the sale.

For example, suppose that a dropshipper started a simple sales website called Thermal Bottles. Thermal Bottles offers state of the art, high-quality thermoses and water bottles. The dropshipper has a wholesaler who is willing to provide these water bottles and will fulfill orders for the shipper. When the customer clicks on the buy button on the Thermal Bottles website, the purchase order is then submitted to the wholesaler. The wholesaler then processes the purchase order, charging the dropshipper for the wholesale cost of the product, and then beginning in the shipping process. The customer receives the order and has no idea that their new water bottle was never in possession of Thermal Bottles.

All packaging and contact information sent to the customer is the information that you have provided the wholesaler. So if there is a question or a problem, the dropshipper is the one who is contacted, not the wholesaler. All the wholesaler does is charge you for the discounted price and ship out the product. Your profits will be the markup you've set for your products. So if the wholesaler charges you $1.50 for a water bottle, and you sell it for $2.50, you'll have made a profit of a dollar, minus the fees and other costs associated with making a sale.

To summarize, the dropshipping process is simple: you charge a customer for a product, then place the order on their behalf to a supplier, who charges you a discounted wholesale rate. The supplier handles the shipping and you handle the branding, storefront and customer service. You make a profit off of the markup, the supplier makes a profit off of the sale and the customer receives their product. Everyone wins with this model.

You should be able to see that the biggest challenges for a dropshipper is acquiring the right supplier and ensuring that the ordering process goes smoothly. A customer won't care about the wholesaler being the one to screw up the order, it is your company's name on the packaging and it is your company's reputation on the line. We'll cover ways to find good suppliers in a later chapter.

The chain of distribution has multiple points for entry as a dropshipper. Whether it's working with a manufacturer directly, finding a good wholesaler or simply making deal with retail companies who are willing to provide you with their supplies in exchange for orders, you will find that there are unique challenges behind working with any of them. The good news is that customers simply don't care where a product comes from. All they care about is that they have a high-quality product that meets their needs and their expectations. And as long as you find the right suppliers to work with, you should have no trouble achieving this at all.

Chapter 6: Assess Your Sales Channels

Since the role of a dropshipper is unknown, a customer's perception of you will be entirely based on the storefront that you are operating. There are multiple types of sales channels that you can utilize, selling your products on various sales oriented websites or on your own. This chapter will analyze and assess a handful of the most popular platforms to sell dropshipped products on.

Dropshipping on eBay

eBay was once the king of online auctions, especially when it came to finding great deals. As the eBay craze grew, people began to find that they could create functional business on eBay, opting to focus on using Buy It Now functions instead of the traditional bidding model. Over time, eBay because to embrace these uses and worked to create legitimate storefronts, where store owners could sell traditional products in bulk without any bidding aspects whatsoever.

eBay has simple policies on dropshipping. They allow for it, with the caveat that you are still responsible for the quality and safe delivery of the product. So that means your reputation and your rating is on the line when dropping through eBay.

Since people are actively searching on eBay to purchase products, you don't have to worry too much about creating convincing sales pitches. Instead, you just need to create good product descriptions, have a good-looking product and competitive pricing. Customers will find your product just by using eBay's search engine. This can help save money when it comes to advertising initially. However, the drawback here is that you will have trouble creating a strong brand identity and will have to deal with other competitors who are also going to be listed on the search engine. You'll need to work to differentiate your product somehow, which can be tricky since you're selling products that any dropshipper can access.

eBay as a dropshipping platform isn't terribly ideal. You don't have a large degree of control over your storefront and your product is just another product in a sea of searches. Customer acquisition can be harder and you won't be able to build a sufficient relationship with customers through the tools that eBay provides. It can be a good place to work with as a beginner, or if you want to have a larger assortment of products that aren't thematically connected to each other, but for the most part, eBay doesn't provide you with the options to be a serious dropshipper.

Dropshipping on Amazon

Amazon is another simple platform to use, although it is quite similar to using eBay in disadvantage. Their policies allow for dropshipping, as long as you only use your own information in the packaging. You cannot have any information about the wholesaler or manufacturer within your packaging. Otherwise, you are free to dropship with them.

Amazon isn't ideal as a platform either. The lack of having a distinct brand identity and instead just being a result in a search means you won't be able to form meaningful relationships with your customers. Customer acquisition is useful, but customer retention is extremely important. If you can retain a high number of your customers, you will be able to sell plenty of products to them. However, this requires a personal relationship and a connection, one that is often fostered through brand identity. Amazon doesn't provide you with the tools to create a solid sales platform that will generate repeat business.

Dropshipping on Shopify

Shopify makes for one of the better sales platforms due to the fact that they offer you the ability to create your own sales websites. Good dropshipping is all about creating a particular brand identity, one that will resonate with consumers and help create connections. Shopify is a sales oriented website, offering you all the options you need to create a beautiful and functional online storefront.

In addition to the ability to customize the look and feel of your website, Shopify offers tools and apps that will aid you directly in your dropshipping endeavors. There are apps that will even assist in automating shipping, which helps reduce one of the more exhaustive tasks within the dropshipping world.

The major drawback to using Shopify is that you're responsible for every aspect of your website's creation. You're going to have to work to create a good visual brand, which often translates to spending time and maybe even money on finding premium themes for your website. You'll need to write all of the ad copy yourself, work on the SEO to improve search results and manage every aspect of the sales process. Shopify will offer you plenty of tools to use it effectively, but you will have to put in the majority of the work yourself.

There is also a monthly cost to Shopify, as well as a credit card fee to account for as well. But these costs are just part of running an online storefront. You won't be able to avoid paying fees for just about any online sales services out there.

Where Shopify excels is in the ability for you to distinguish your own company and create your own brand identity. Customers will return to a fully functional website and will be able to see all the products that you have to offer them. You can upsell, you can directly market through Facebook ads and you can even create your own coupons to incentivize sales. These controls are invaluable for customer acquisition and retention.

Another big benefit behind Shopify is that it is really focused on people who just want to create effective sales websites. If you don't want to go through the headache of creating your own website, using a content management system like WordPress, then you should seriously consider using Shopify. The price point is well worth what you get in return.

Alternative Sales Channels

The top three websites mentioned are what most people think when they consider dropshipping. And while it is true that all three websites are vehicles for sales, they aren't the only platforms that exist. You have other options, such as creating your own website, using a CMS like WordPress or Squarespace.

Creating your own website from scratch gives you unrestricted freedom, where you can do just about anything you like, but there are higher costs. You'll need to either spend money to have the website built by a developer, or you'll need to make one yourself. There is a lot that goes into the principles of building a good website, so unless you want to become educated in that field, you'd be better of going with a developer who can make a functional website that looks good and works well.

Other options include using a Shopify competitor such as WooCommerce. There are dozens of alternative channels out there to consider, and honestly, they aren't terribly different from each other. As long as you have the creative freedoms to create connection with your customers and methods of retaining them, you should be fine. Look for the platform that works best for you and don't worry about the competitors. When you're just getting started all you really need is something simple and functional.

Chapter 7: Researching a Niche and Selecting Products

Once you've figured out what kind of platform you want to sell on, you're going to need products to sell. Thanks to the wide variety of wholesalers that exist and the small-time manufacturers, there really is no shortage of different products that you can sell on your storefront. However, if you want customers to buy what you're selling, you must first identify their market needs. And since the online marketplace is huge, the best way to ensure you will actually make sales, you must identify a product niche.

What is a Niche?

A nice is a specialty, a small corner of the market that is hyper targeted to a smaller group of people. In the gigantic world of online business, you simply won't make money selling generalized products. Firstly, you won't be able to beat the prices that large box stores put forth, and second, you won't be able to get people to visit your website for those products. Large, wildly popular products already have established markets and brand identities. You won't be able to crack that market from the outside.

Instead, a good dropshipper is able to identify a niche market, a market that has a demand for a very specific type of product, a product that isn't widely sold. A niche is how you will make money as a dropshipper. If you are able to identify a niche market that is untapped or has low levels of competition, you will be able to find a group of buyers who will be more likely to purchase your products.

The trick then, is to figure out how to find a niche market. Consumer tastes are constantly changing and evolving. If you are able to identify an underserved market and create a strong brand identity, you can do very well for yourself. But it will require a serious amount of market research before you are able to determine which products you should sell.

How to do Niche Research

Niche research simply requires you to use a combination of tools and search engine results to try and accurately predict an underserved area of the market. There is a bit of luck involved with this process, as finding niches is difficult. It's a bit like searching for oil. You use the proper tools to gauge interest, you survey the area, but you won't really know if you've made any money until you start drilling.

Fortunately, with the amount of data that is captured through search engines such as Google and Amazon, we are able to use tools to sift through and find untapped markets. You will want to use specialized tools, such as Google Trends to see what people are searching for. The more you dig into these searches, you'll be able to observe what results a person receives when typing a search term.

For example, if you find that people are heavily searching for red water bottles, you'll be able to search for yourself and see what the results are. If there is a heavy amount of competition in that field, you haven't found a strong enough niche. What makes for a good niche is a combination of high demand and low market supply. The less competition that exists in the field, the easier it will be to break in. The higher the competition, the lower the profit margins as well as the lower the chance of you getting a customer's attention.

How to Use the Graphs and Data from Google Trends

Search results are essential for identifying a niche market to enter. Consumers find products through multiple methods, such as word of mouth, direct marketing or typing keywords in a search engine. By following how many people are typing in specific keywords in relation to a product, we can track what the interest level in a specific field is. Google Trends tracks these searches and creates graphs for us to be able to analyze, displaying interest over time. Here, you'll not only be able to follow how things are trending, but you'll also be able to see how they have trended over time.

This data is invaluable when it comes to tracking how a niche can potentially perform. A niche that is steadily rising over the years indicates that there is growth in the sector, which you want, since more customers equal more sales. A search trend that shows dwindling or minimal results over time indicates that consumer tastes are changing and as such, investing time and energy in selling those niche products might not bring back any returns.

Accessing Google Trends is as simple as going to trends.google.com. From there, you'll be able to type in search terms and see how they are trending. In addition to the trends, you'll be able to see search terms that are related, either similar topics or search terms that yield more focused results.

Of course, using Google Trends can be a little time consuming, as you will be required to type in search results by hand. This means that you are essentially going to be guessing about potential products to sell and then sorting through the results to see if there are trends moving in a positive direction. Still, this research is invaluable. If you are able to locate one niche market that is starved for good products, you can make a killing.

How to Use Google Keyword Tools for Niche Research

Google has a keyword planner program that can be accessed as long as you have a Google Ads account. Creating an Ads account is free to do and doesn't take much time, so you should create one if you don't have one already. Once you've made the ad account, you'll be able to access their keyword planner program, a powerful search engine that lets you see how specific keywords are performing. This is a more focused version than Google Trends, which only provides with overviews. By using Google Keyword Planner, you'll be able to see suggestions for specific keywords, based on the terms you give them, the number of engagement that consumers have with those keywords and the amount of competition for those keywords.

This will help you when bouncing around different ideas for finding a niche market. You can also see what the cost of specific ad types are as well, which can help you when it comes to advertising for your company later on.

Ultimately, niche research takes time and effort. Tracking down the best possible niches isn't easy, but when you find the right market, you will be rewarded with a higher level of sales than if you were to enter into a saturated market.

Things to Look Out for When Selecting Products

Once you've gotten a handle on how to research niche products and have found a few different areas that look promising, you'll need to make the decision on which products that you want to sell. This is trickier than it sounds because you're not reliant on your own production capabilities, instead, you'll have to go out and actually find suppliers who will provide those products for you. This means that you won't always find a proper niche market that also aligns with the dropshipping system.

Other things to consider when selecting products:

- **Staying Power**: You want to find a product that isn't a fad, or won't just simply drop out of public consciousness quickly. A good product is one that will stay in demand for a long time.

- **Repeat purchases**: A great product is one that the consumer will want to purchase more of. Having a single sale is nice, but repeat businesses is invaluable to the

53

growth of your dropshipping company. So make sure that the product you select can be bought again and again by the same customer, as this will help increase your profit margins greatly.

- **Price Point:** There are plenty of things that can prevent a customer from clicking on the buy button, and price can certainly be one of those barriers. When you're just starting out, you might want to consider focusing on selling lower priced products, as opposed to products that have a higher premium. This isn't to say that high-end products don't sell, it can just be easier to sell cheaper products at the beginning. Then, as you learn effective marketing and sales techniques, you can start offering higher prices.

Measuring Competition

Competition is virtually impossible to escape when dropshipping. The fact that anyone can access suppliers that offer similar products means you will invariably deal with rival websites. However, you should work to mitigate competition as much as possible when selecting a product. If the competition is too strong you will be forced to price competitively and this can translate to razor thin margins.

Finding competition is fairly simple. All you need to do is run a web search of the products you're thinking about selling and then estimating the number of direct results that you are seeing. Then, spend some time investigating these websites to determine how strong of a competitor they are to you. Here are some questions to ask as you evaluate the top search results of each field.

What is the quality of their website?

Website quality is a big deal when it comes to competition. A hard to navigate, low-functioning website that makes purchasing items difficult can easily be beaten by someone with a sleek, high functioning website. Users are looking for good experiences and can quickly be off-put by something as simple as visual design. The speed that a website takes to load, the visual brand and the navigation all make up the quality of a niche website. If you find that competitors have ugly, poor functioning or slow loading websites, this can signal an area that you can break into. Since you're essentially selling the same products, things like user experience have a higher premium to customers.

What are customers saying?

Product reviews will help you gauge how your competition is functioning. If you notice middling reviews or even a wide outcrop of negative feedback, you have the potential to get ahead of these competitors. Identify what these complaints are and then figure out how you can solve them. If all goes well, you should be able to use that higher level of quality to muscle your way up higher in the rankings.

What incentives are they offering?

Incentives are a major part of creating a sales relationship with new customers. It's rather hard to convince a customer to click the buy button, especially if they are working with this brand for the first time. In order to assist the customer in purchasing, most good sales companies will create incentives. Whether it's new user discounts, free shipping or free samples, most companies rely on incentive to create that pivotal first step. Try to identify what incentives, if any, that these competitors are offering. Extremely attractive incentives may end up being too costly for you to compete with, if that's the case you might want to consider moving towards a different niche. Conversely, weak or non-existent incentives signal that if you move into that territory, you could potentially convert more customers than your competitor.

What prices are they charging?

This is the big one. Pricing comes from a combination of demand and competition. A business will try to make as much profit as they can, however, competition often pushes the prices lower. Two businesses must match each other's prices if they are competing for the same client and offering the same product. This lowers the price to the lowest possible profit margin.

High markups can signal low amount of market competition. If you know that a water bottle sells wholesale for 1.00 and you see a competitor selling it for $7.00, that can signal that the market isn't terribly competitive in that area. Or, it might even show that this store has a significant market share. If that's the case, moving in with competitive prices will help divert sales away from your competitor and bring them straight to you.

Conversely, you will be able to tell that if prices are extremely close to the wholesale value that you might as well not bother entering that field. It has already been too saturated and you will fight to find a voice in the market.

What is the advertising cost for this product?

While this isn't directly related to competition websites, it is an important question to ask. Paid advertising is a necessity in the online world of marketing. One way you can analyze the level of competition in a field is to see how much advertising of a niche market will cost with pay-per-click ads through either Google or Facebook. High bidding costs indicate that there is a steady stream of advertisers who are all trying to outbid each other for the attention of your target market. Low bidding costs mean that there isn't a large amount of demand, indicating that you could potentially break into that market with lower levels of competition.

Find a Niche Where You Can Add Value to the Product

One last thought on finding a niche is to remember that the goal of all sales is to solve a problem. Someone, somewhere has a problem and they need that problem to be solved. Your products are the solution to that problem and as such, a customer will be motivated to make the purchase. One of the most important things to keep in mind as you search for a niche is that you want to be able to find some way to add value to the product. Whether that value is something intangible, like quality customer service, or more concrete, such as higher quality, you will want to find some way that you can add value to the product. Sometimes all it takes is the willingness to listen to potential customers and find what needs they have in relation to the product.

For example, in observing product reviews, you find that most customers want a wider variety of colors. Simply by finding a supplier who can provide that level of variety may be all it takes to increase sales and differentiate yourself from other competitors. This requires creativity and the willingness to look for ways to make your customers happier with your product. The more you can set your products apart from other dropshipping companies, the more of a relationship you'll be able to build with customers. The stronger the relationship, the better the chance of word of mouth marketing *and* repeat orders!

At the end of it all, one of the most difficult tasks in dropshipping is finding the right product to sell. Market research is difficult and, for all of your efforts, there is a chance that you might simply not have picked the right product. The good news here is that even if you aren't able to find a good niche the first few times, your investment was minimal and you won't have to worry about a large warehouse full of purchased supplies just sitting around.

So be patient with yourself, spend as much time as you need in the research phase and don't be afraid to go back to the drawing board if things don't work out. If you keep at it, eventually you will find a rewarding niche that will bring in the sales you're looking for. It just takes time and dedication.

Chapter 8: Looking for Suppliers and Manufacturers

How to Find Suppliers

Once the long task of market research has been finished, you'll need to go about finding suppliers who can fulfill the orders that you will be bringing in. Finding a good supplier isn't easy and it takes a lot of thorough searching before you can find the ones that are right for you.

As mentioned before, there are two primary types of suppliers, wholesalers and manufacturers. Finding a manufacturer who is willing to work with you directly will be rare and is not recommended for those who are just starting out. The reason for this is that manufacturers are often looking for large orders and you simply won't' be able to fulfill those minimum order requirements when you are in the beginning phases. Rather, we would suggest that you focus instead on finding a wholesaler who is equipped and capable of fulfilling orders that you place with them.

How do you find a wholesaler?

The most tried and true way to find a wholesaler is to start with the manufacturer. Once you've identified the product that you want to sell, look up manufacturers who create said product. From there, reach out to the manufacturer and find out who they distribute their products to. By following these leads, you'll be able to identify the wholesalers that purchase these products and store them. Then, it's simply a matter of contacting those wholesalers directly and working out a deal with them.

Another method would be to use internet searches to find them. But you should be careful when taking this route, as there are plenty of websites out there that aren't actually wholesalers, but rather scammers looking to take advantage of new dropshippers. We'll cover how to spot fake wholesalers below.

Or, if you want to use a direct website that focuses on matching business with suppliers, you may want to consider using Alibaba. Alibaba helps connect dropshippers to suppliers in places such as China. Of course, there are risks when working with some of the suppliers, as their quality and standards can be lower. This isn't to say there aren't good suppliers on Alibaba, but you should exercise caution while searching for suppliers with them.

How to spot fake wholesalers

Unfortunately, like any endeavor, there are pitfalls to be wary of. One such pitfall in finding a good supplier is that there are companies out there who pretend to be wholesalers, when in truth they are actually dropshippers in disguise. They offer you product rates that are actually marked up and then fulfill your orders through their own wholesaler, taking the lion's share of the profits. You and the customer won't know the difference, since they simply submit *your* purchase orders to *their* wholesalers.

This can be a frustrating situation to be in, since it will cut into your margins significantly. Fortunately, there are ways that you can spot these situations. The first way is simple prevention. By following a manufacturer's distribution list, you won't run the risk of finding a supplier who is a dropshipper in disguise.

Another giveaway that you're working with a false wholesaler is if they are eager to collect fees from you. By charging a monthly "user fee" or "service charges," they are really just looking to add more money to their bottom line. Wholesalers don't make money off of charging dropshipper service fees, they make their money off of selling their products. Be leery of wholesalers that are looking to pad their pockets with your money upfront. Most of the time they aren't legitimate.

Another sign of a scam is if the wholesaler is also directly selling their products to consumers. Wholesalers don't deal with consumers, that is the job of the retailer. If you find yourself on a wholesale site that sells and ships products straight to consumers, with no minimum orders, chances are you're just on a dropshipper's website.

Other types of scams that a wholesaler may attempt would be to charge you upfront for the cost of the product and then fail to ship out the product when you place the order. This leads to a terrible customer service experience as well as a refund request, which comes out of your pocket. Often times, these false wholesalers will simply just vanish or refused to reply to you. This is why it's important to get a sense for the physical location of the wholesaler. If you can get good contact information, have a few phone conversations with the individual or otherwise confirm that they do exist and they are who they say they are, you'll be fine. But if you find that contacting anyone in the organization is hard or that they only exist through email, chances are rather high that they are just a fraudster.

You'll need to exercise caution and stay sharp when searching for wholesalers online. Don't rush into anything headlong, instead, take your time and do your research. If you sense that something may be amiss, or the fees being charged are simply too high, you could possibly be dealing with a scammer. Take your time and do your due diligence.

Contacting the Supplier

Once you've identified the supplier(s) that you wish to work with, you're going to need to contact them and convince them to work with you. One of the big advantages of dropshipping growing in popularity is the fact that most suppliers understand how it works and are agreeable to working with new customers, as this expands their ability to make sales. However, just because you call them up and tell them that you're a dropshipper doesn't mean they will automatically trust you.

You'll need to verify that you are a legitimate business and this often involves showing them that you are incorporated, that you have a business plan, etc. These are simple steps that will help them know that you aren't just some random person trying to get cheaper products by skipping the retailers.

Wholesalers often have sales departments who are in charge of assisting potential clients in setting up accounts with them, so you'll most likely be working with them. Make sure that you are to the point, you don't ask too many questions and signal that the reason you are contacting them is that you are ready to act. A wholesaler isn't interested in helping an entrepreneur start their new business, they are interested in making sales.

There may be some negotiations or convincing required, especially if the wholesaler doesn't have a regular amount of dropshippers that they work with. If this is the case, be as patient as possible and don't make major demands. Instead, work to show them how your business model will aid them in making money and be direct about your goals.

One thing to keep in mind is that when you first begin working with a wholesaler, even in the preliminary phase, you are starting a new relationship. The relationship at first will be shaky and untested. Don't add unnecessary stress by attempting to negotiate discounts or get some kind of deal for yourself. Most wholesalers aren't looking to just cut their rates with someone unproven. Once you have a track record and show that not only do you provide sales but you're also reliable, it will be a different story. But in the beginning, you have little to go on other than your words, so make sure that you use them wisely!

Another thing to take note of is the fact that emails aren't nearly as effective as phone calls when it comes to first impressions. An email can quickly be swept aside, but a phone conversation, even a short one can make a good enough impression on the person in charge of dropshipping accounts. By creating that human connection, you will increase your chances of getting an account with the supplier and most importantly, establish a good relationship from day number one.

Paying Your Supplier

The supplier is paid whenever you place an order with them, charging your credit card on file. This means that you will need to have a business card that has enough of a balance to be able to pay for orders as they come in. Another option, is to simply receive an invoice from the supplier, paying them for the orders you've made within X amount of days, based on the terms that you've worked out with the supplier. The only problem here is that if you're just starting out and you don't have any credibility, most suppliers will want to see the money up front. There's no reason they should be giving what basically amounts to a loan to someone they don't have a strong relationship with, so you'll most likely need to wait until they trust you enough to give you invoice privileges.

Signs of a Good Supplier

You don't want to just settle with the first supplier that you come across. Like all markets, there is competition within the supplier world as well, and you'll want to pick the competitors who offer you the best value. With that in mind, let's look at a few signs of a good supplier.

Clear Understanding of Dropshipping

With dropshipping growing as an industry, you'll want to work with suppliers who have a clear understanding of who you are. This will help you tremendously when it comes to getting them to agree to work with you, as they won't be surprised by the model you're describing. On top of that, if they understand and work with dropshippers regularly, they'll most likely be equipped to take on new dropshippers. This translates to a higher level of support when it comes to questions on your end.

Quality Shipping and Handling

You'll want to ensure that these suppliers are competent at the most important part of their role: shipping and handling. You can test this by making a few orders on your own, to see not only the quality of the products, but also the speed of their shipping and if they are accurate. You don't want to end up working with a supplier that is frequently shipping the wrong product, nor do you want to deal with one that drags their feet when it comes to getting the product shipped on time.

Accessibility

A good supplier is well equipped to be accessible through the use of modern technology. For example, you'll want a supplier who will take orders through email, instead of just manual orders submitted over the phone. Those who use automation and data tracking will be easier to work with, especially once you start scaling your business.

Supplier Directories

The last option that you have in your search for a supplier is to use what is known as a directory. A directory holds a large catalog of different suppliers, providing you with the contact information as well as summaries so you can get in touch with them. The downsides to using a directory is that you often have to pay a fee in order to use their service. However, these directories can be extremely invaluable, especially if you are struggling to find suppliers through manufacturers.

It's important to make sure that you have properly researched the directory before you purchase their services. The last thing you want is to end up buying a directory list that has useless or outdated information. Doing a quick search online about the directory should provide you with just about everything you need to know about their trustworthiness.

Here is a list of a few trustworthy supplier directories that we have compiled:

1. Oberlo
2. Worldwide Brands
3. Alibaba
4. SaleHoo
5. Wholesale Central

Ultimately, after you've found a supplier that is willing to work with you, you'll be just about ready to get started with your dropshipping company. Of course, when you're just starting out, it can be a bit overwhelming or intimidating to pick up the phone and try to convince suppliers to work with you. The good news is that with each phone call that you make, you'll get better and better, until having these discussions will be second nature. The only thing that you need to focus on is to keep at it until you have all the suppliers that you need for your business!

Chapter 9: Handling Inventory and Multiple Suppliers

Inventory management is an important piece of the dropshipping puzzle. You'll need to keep a close eye on how much inventory you have available. Shortages can threaten to disrupt your business, and the last thing that you want is to take a large order without the ability to fulfill it properly!

Best Practices for Inventory Management

The first thing that you'll want to do once you have established a dropshipping relationship with a supplier is to gain access to product data. This data will be necessary for you to keep track of things such as UPCs, inventory amount and the current price of those products. A good supplier will have a way to receive frequent updates of this data, either through sending automated daily emails or even through hourly online updates. You will need this data in order to monitor how things are going on the inventory end of things.

Fortunately, there are plenty of online services out there that will offer you inventory monitoring software. This software is often able to take any type of data provided by the supplier and extrapolate all of the important and pertinent details for you to see at a glance. On top of that, you can receive alerts, synchronize across different platforms and receive up-to-date information about what products have been shipping. You'll want to find the right kind of software to use, depending on the type of platform you are using. Shopify, for example, has inventory management apps that will provide you with the pivotal information, in exchange for a fee.

Synching inventory data with your supplier is pivotal. If your current online inventory doesn't reflect what your supplier has, it means customers can order more than you can supply.

Don't balk at the idea of paying for inventory management services, as these are simply just another cost of doing business. While it possible for you to manually analyze your inventory using the data provided by your supplier, this often takes quite a bit of time. Automation always pays off in the long run, because it frees you up to spend more time on the important stuff.

How to manage multiple suppliers

Working with one supplier is complicated enough, but working with multiple suppliers can be a bit overwhelming if you don't have a properly designed system. Ideally, you'll want to try and find a single supplier who is able to supply all of the products that you want to sell. This is most beneficial because it allows for you to bundle products together and ship them to the same house.

For example, if a customer buys a water bottle and a steel thermos from your storefront, if they are both sold by the same supplier, both products will be packaged and shipped together, saving money on shipping. However, if the water bottle is owned by supplier A and the thermos is from supplier B, things get much more complicated.

The first option would be to just ship separately. This means that you send purchase orders to both suppliers. But before you are able to do that, you'll need to have some way of identifying which product is owned by which supplier. Normally this is done with an SKU, or stock keeping unit, an ID code that will let you know which company owns which. You'll have to input your own SKU's for each product in your inventory, so that you can quickly tell which products are owned by which company.

For example, if you sell water bottles from Supplier A and thermoses from Supplier B, you would need to distinguish each product's owner by using a unique SKU code. Supplier A could simply be labeled ASKU and Supplier B would be BSKU. This means that when you see BSKU150, you know that the product is owned by supplier B, just from looking at the SKU number.

A good inventory management system will help to distinguish between multiple suppliers. Without taking the time to ensure that each product you sell has an SKU number that is unique to the supplier, you run the risk of accidentally sending orders to the wrong supplier. They won't know the difference and ship the product like they would any other order, sending the customer the wrong supplies.

How to Deal with Out of Stock Orders

Out of Stock orders can be a real problem if you aren't careful. The best way to deal with an out stock order is to simply prevent it. In order to prevent running out of stock, you'll want to find a backup supplier who offers the same product that your current supplier does. That way, if your primary supplier runs out of stock and you have a few orders slip in, you'll still be able to fulfill by sending those orders to your backup. This will help avoid a crisis and will keep things running smoothly.

Tight monitoring and control of your inventory data will also help prevent orders from occurring when you are out of stock. Being able to identify when a product's stock is running low or empty will allow for you to quickly update the store page, preventing customers from clicking on the buy button. Of course, if you're stopping customers from making purchases, you're losing out on money, so this should be avoided if possible.

Yet, there may be times when the worst of the worst happens. For some reason, your supplier is out of stock and twenty customers have already paid to have the item sent to their homes. What is there to do in these situations? You have a few options

Move Quickly

If you find yourself suddenly dealing with an order for a product you don't have, it is possible for you to try and move quickly to source from another supplier. This will require you to move as fast as possible, and may be a long shot, but you can get lucky. Always make sure that you have a list of suppliers who do offer either identical or similar products so you can source from them.

Contact the customer

If it becomes clear that you aren't able to fulfill the order within the window that you have for shipping, you'll have to contact the customer and provide them with options. In general, contacting them via phone would be more personal than email, and if you must email them, please don't send a generic looking email. This will only cause more damage. Instead, you'll want to try and be honest and personal, inform them of the mistake that was made and then see what you can do to make it right. Try offering a similar product, or give them a discount on something a little more expensive than their current order. This is really a customer service challenge. If you're willing to show them that you are penitent and that you want to make things right for them, they will see you as more than just another faceless company.

Will some people be upset? Certainly, but those who aren't angry with you may end up thankful for your honesty and willingness to help them. Shortages happen sometimes and it isn't the end of the world. What is most important in these situations is that customers feel heard and cared for. As long as you are able to achieve that, you might be able to retain their business.

Prepare to refund

You will most likely need to refund your customers in these situations. Be ready for it. Don't give the customer a hard time, nor try to obfuscate the problem with meaningless promises such as "it'll ship soon, I promise." Instead, just take the hit and move on. You'll need to focus more on creating a faster inventory management system in order to avoid these shortages again.

Inventory management is serious business. Automation tools are your biggest friend in this field, as it will help you keep a close eye on pricing and shortages, preventing customer service disasters and aiding you in the shipping process. Don't let your desire to hold onto a few bucks a month keep you from using some of the most powerful tools out there. You will save a lot more money in the long run by using them.

Chapter 10: Handling Security and Fraud Issues

The internet can be a nasty place sometimes. There are thieves, hackers and scammers about who look for ways to make money off of the weakness of others. As a business, you'll need to ensure that your website is secure as well as ensure you have methods handling fraud and hackers attempting to steal customer data. The last thing you want is to enable these thieves from causing damage to both you and your customers.

How to Deal with Fraudulent Orders

Miss Agatha Maple buys $300 worth of products from you one day and that is cause to celebrate! But before you pop the champaign, you realize that a chargeback has been initiated. When contacting the credit card company, you discover that Agatha's credit card number had been stolen and the products were fraudulently ordered. Now, you've lost the products and will still have to pay your supplier for what has been purchased.

This is more common than you think. Identity thieves often try to buy products using credit card numbers as quickly as they can. Their goal is to beat the credit card companies from halting the transaction. As long as they can get you to ship the products out, they've won. In order to prevent this from happening, you will need to take a few simple steps to filter out frauds.

The first step is to make sure that you have proper verification systems in place. Things such as requiring security code confirmation from the back of credit cards can help reduce the number of fraudulent transactions. Verification software and security programs can also be of assistance. Some will even provide you with financial protection in the cases of fraud.

Once you have a verification system in place, you should be insulated. However, it is still important to recognize the signs of potential fraud, just in case someone manages to slip through the cracks.

1. **Different shipping address from billing.**

Fraudsters will use the billing address of the credit card number that they've stolen, but will redirect the goods to be sent to a different address. In some cases, they may end up calling or sending an email, asking for the original shipping address to be changed and directed elsewhere. These aren't always thieves, but it should raise a red flag for you

2. **High orders and rush shipping**

An expensive order combined with rush shipping may indicate the potential for fraud. Remember, the fraudster is trying to get the products as quickly as he can in order to avoid having the card shut down by the bank or the credit card company. If you notice an unusually high order combined with the fastest possible shipping, this is cause for concern.

3. **International orders**

While not all international orders are signals for fraud or scams, if you notice that the billing address doesn't match the country of destination, then there is a significant chance of fraud.

Handling Suspected Cases of Fraud

If you suspect that an order may be fraudulent, you'll want to contact the customer as soon as possible. Call or email them and begin a verification process to see if they are indeed who they claim to be. Don't be afraid to do your due diligence. Most customers are understanding about fraud prevention, so don't worry about offending them. It is better to save yourself the trouble and the money by checking in with the customer than to lose all the money over the fear of offending someone.

Ensuring the Credit Card Numbers of Your Customers are Safe and Secure

Data theft is growing to be more commonplace online. Large companies such as Equifax have learned the hard way that if they don't protect their data, they can end up dealing with severe consequences. Fortunately, protecting your customer's information isn't too difficult.

You'll want to ensure first of all that your website is secured. If you're running off a platform such as Shopify, you don't need to worry about the security, as that comes automatically. However, if you are running your own website off a CMS, you'll need to ensure that it has an SSL certificate and that you have installed the proper security measures to protect a data breach from occurring.

Most credit card processing services are secured by default (and by law) so you don't have to worry about breaches as long as you are working with a trusted processing service that has guarantees of security. Always do your research and make sure that you are working with approved processors.

Prevention is really the best way to ensure that you don't fall victim to fraudulent purchases. Nothing can be worse than losing both money and a product to a thief who's using someone else's credit card. However, by having a strong prevention system in place and ensuring that there is some level of verification before shipping a product, you can make it harder for a thief to take advantage of you. Remember, thieves and crooks are often looking for the path of least resistance. A single verification attempt may end up shaking them away from their attempts and leaving your website alone. Pay attention and make sure that whenever you see strange or out of character orders, that you verify the purchase with the customer.

Chapter 11: Avoiding Chargebacks

While fraud may be one of the major causes behind a chargeback, it's not the only reason. Sometimes a customer can be quite unhappy with your business and as a result, will try to initiate a chargeback with their credit card company. A chargeback is most unfortunate because not only do you have to pay back what you charged the customer, but you are also hit with a fee from the credit card company or bank.

Needless to say, chargebacks are not good for your business in any way. If you want to avoid chargebacks, you'll need to understand the legitimate uses of such a thing and what would lead a customer to make such a decision.

Legitimate Chargebacks:

A chargeback is a legal way to get money back from a dishonest merchant. It was created as a method of consumer defense, able to protect consumers from being taken advantage of by shady business owners. The ability to contact your bank or credit card company and issue a chargeback at any time keeps most merchants honest. There are a few legitimate reasons that a customer can initiate a chargeback:

1. Fraudulent Purchases

We've already covered this, but chargebacks are a form of fraud protection, meant to ensure that the customer's credit card information is safe in the hands of a merchant. If a merchant uses that card number to charge more, the customer can initiate a chargeback.

2. Bad Purchase

A bad purchase can be defined as any time a customer acquires a product and realizes that they were misled in some way. Perhaps the product is shoddy, low quality and doesn't work. Maybe the product arrives in shambles or perhaps it doesn't even arrive at all. Either way, a bad purchase gives a customer a legitimate right to initiate a chargeback. If you lied to them, took advantage or in any way misled them, you could be on the hook for a chargeback.

Illegitimate Chargebacks

While the two types of chargebacks above are considered legitimate, there is also a host of illegitimate reason for chargebacks. Reasons can include: attempting to keep both the product and the money they paid, realizing they didn't want the product but used it anyway and can't get a refund, shipping took too long, they didn't like the product as much as they thought, etc.

Illegitimate chargebacks do happen and there are avenues for you to dispute a chargeback with a bank or credit card company, but in doing so, you are wasting a large amount of your valuable time. Chargebacks can be contested successfully, but you'll need to have proper documentation in order to do so.

Preventing Chargebacks

Having a chargeback show up at your door is painful. It will result in financial loss and if you aren't careful, you might even end up suspended from a bank or credit card company's services. This could potentially result in you becoming blacklisted! The best way to avoid a chargeback is to work to create a strong customer service base that actively solves customer problems.

If a customer is unhappy with a product, they will need an avenue to vent that frustration. Their first stop should be opening a communication channel with you. It is paramount that you have avenues for them to be able to contact you quickly and easily.

A money back guarantee or a satisfaction promise is often good enough to get the dialogue going with the customer. This can open up the discussion and help you solve your customer's problem. Sometimes their complaints are quite legitimate, perhaps something went wrong in the shipping process, or maybe the product's quality was low. If that's the case, you can work to make things right, which will prevent them from initiating a chargeback. Having to issue a refund is much more ideal than paying for both the chargeback and the fees associated with them.

If the customer's problem doesn't seem legitimate, or warrants pause when considering a refund, you'll want to make sure that you properly document their complaints, so you can refer to them later if they end up initiating a chargeback. Still, you should ask if issuing a refund or finding some other way to make them happy would result in more sales from them. Good customer service sometimes means biting the bullet so that the customer walks away happy. It's really a matter of discretion on your part.

The best way to prevent chargebacks is to communicate clearly about your product and work to ensure that you don't make any false claims. Don't give your customers any potential ammunition that they can use against you. Make sure that your product quality is up to par and keep an eye on any potential shipping delays, ensuring that you keep a clear line of communication to the customer.

Chapter 12: Handling Product Returns and Shipping Problems

There are times when a customer decides they want to return the product in exchange for a refund. Perhaps they received the wrong product, or the quality wasn't what they were expecting. In these cases, you'll need to understand how the return process works.

The Return Process

Ultimately, a return means that a product will be sent back to you or the supplier in exchange for a refund. However, a supplier most likely has its own terms and conditions on how they handle returns, including their refund policy. Some won't refund past a certain point of time, such as thirty days, and others may not accept returns outside of specific parameters, such as damaged goods.

It is important for you to be aware of your supplier's return policies and that your own return policies are similar, so that you two are working on the same clock. You don't want to have a 15 day return policy when your supplier only has a 7 day policy, because if the customer tries to return on day 10, you'll have to eat the cost.

It isn't unreasonable to expect that a supplier will refund the cost of the product, but they may require some convincing. If you have a good relationship with the supplier, this shouldn't be a trouble, but if you are working with a supplier who is strict or returns averse, you might find this to be a little more difficult. Regardless, if the return was due to a mistake on the suppliers part, they should be expected to pay for it.

However, regardless of whether the supplier is willing to pay for the return or not, the customer won't know the difference. In their eyes, they are only dealing with one entity: your company. This means that at the end of the day, the responsibility for the return and the refund fall on your shoulders. You can't just tell a customer you can't accept a return of a defective product because of your supplier, this would be frustrating and could potentially lose you a customer. Instead, you'll have to work to make it right no matter what, even if it involves taking a hit.

Of course, if that ends up happening, you'll most likely want to rethink your relationship with the supplier.

The process of a return is simple enough. The customer will contact you about a return and you'll verify that they indeed can ship back the product. Then, you will contact the supplier to get what's known as a Return Merchant Authorization number, which is what the customer will put on the package when they ship it back. They then ship the package to the supplier, the supplier refunds you the money and then you refund the customer.

There may be costs associated with a return. Some suppliers charge restocking fees as a means of keeping returns to a minimum. Sometimes you can work to avoid paying a restocking fee, especially if the product was defective or wrong, but most of the time you'll just have to eat the cost.

Another fee associated with returns is the cost of shipping the product back. Most customers won't like the idea of having to spend their own money to get a refund, and since the mistake was on you or the supplier, it really shouldn't be their responsibility. Eating the cost of shipping by sending them a label to print isn't just kind, it's also great customer service. Hopefully this should more than rectify the situation and set their frustrations at ease.

When Does a Return Happen?

A return occurs whenever the customer has found reason enough to send the product back. Either they got the wrong product, the quality was bad or some other issue prompted them to return the product back to you. If this is the case, then you might want to consider sending them your own address for returning the product, so that you can examine what is wrong. This might give you a clue into how to prevent this from occurring more in the future.

Dealing with Shipping Issues

Shipping problems can crop up from time to time, but there's no reason to worry. The world of shipping is in a constant state of flux, so you're going to often deal with these problems. Here are a few different problems that you may face with shipping and ways to solve them.

1. Delayed Shipping

The order went through, the customer has been charged, but for some reason there was a delay in shipping. A delayed shipping situation can be frustrating for a customer, especially if they've paid for expedited shipping or are expecting to see their product within the projected time frame.

The biggest way to handle delayed shipping is to work to find out what is slowing things down and then ensuring that the product is shipped out. If you don't receive confirmation from your supplier after you sent in an order, chances are something may have slipped through the cracks. Be proactive and check in to ensure things are moving along smoothly.

If for some unavoidable reason that shipping has been delayed, the best option would be to contact the customer as soon as possible and inform them about the delay. The customer won't be thrilled, but information is key to reducing anxiety with a customer. Someone who is using your company for the first time might grow nervous after a few days of no confirmation, so you'll want to keep them informed as much as possible.

2. **The customer never received their package**

This can be a real pain, because it requires some detective work. Determining why a customer didn't receive their package means that you'll need to spend time sifting through the chain of distribution. Did the customer accidentally submit the wrong address? Did you somehow make a mistake or did the supplier send the package to the wrong customer? There are plenty of reasons as to why a package never arrived at its intended destination. In some cases, the mail carrier themselves might even be the one at fault.

Once you track down who is at fault, you'll need to take steps to resolve the problem. Most of the time, this simply involves shipping a new package to the customer and charging whoever was at fault for the problem. If a customer sent the wrong address, they are at fault and are not entitled to any kind of refund. If it was the supplier or the mail carrier, they'll be expected to pay for the loss. If it was your own, well, you should work to automate the shipping process so that you don't have to worry about these problems from happening.

3. **Repeated Shipping Errors**

Sometimes you may find that your customers are enduring repeated shipping errors. Either the products take far too long to arrive, the quantity of products has been messed up or a host of other shipping problems have occurred. If these incidents are few and far between, you can chalk it up to being nothing more than a simple accident and those happen from time to time. However, if you realize that these shipping errors have become too commonplace, it might be time to rethink your relationship with your supplier.

A supplier is a business partner and should be making your life easier, not harder. If you endure constant shipping problems, it will ultimately cut into your bottom line by injuring your reputation as well as your relationship with customers. If you cannot get a quality customer experience out of your supplier and they won't take steps to fix constant errors, you should look into finding a new supplier. You simply don't need the headache of trying to endure their carelessness.

International Shipments

Dropshipping with a domestic supplier means that they are wiling to ship domestically, but not all suppliers are interested in shipping internationally. There are challenges and problems that are unique to making international shipments, as well as increased costs which can damage your bottom line.

If you want to ship international, you'll need to make sure that the supplier that you're working with has the capacity to do so. If not, you might want to consider finding a supplier that either allows for international shipping *or* is located in another country, where to them they would just be shipping domestically.

International shipping can be expensive, but if a customer is willing to pay those costs, then there is no reason not to offer that option. However, some customers may balk at the idea of paying significantly more because of the price of shipping and as such, may be dissuaded from using your services. If that's the case, it might be better to only offer shipping to the countries that you can provide the lowest costs. You can use software to help calculate the costs of international shipping and determine which methods of shipment will provide you with the lowest rates.

Shipping requires constant care and monitoring if you want to ensure that your customers end up happy. Part of the dropshpping process is solving the complexities of shipping issues and working to stay ahead of the game. As long as you are willing to keep a close eye on the status of your products and work to resolve return issues as quickly as possible, business should continue moving along quite smoothly.

Chapter 13: Common Dropshipping Pitfalls

By now, we've covered all of the basic points of establishing a dropshipping business. Picking a niche, finding a supplier and creating a storefront to sell wares are all necessary parts of the puzzle. These three elements are easy enough to learn, but require a lot of time and energy to master properly. But as far as preparedness goes, once you have a strong enough understanding of these elements, you should be able to get started!

You'll learn the most simply by doing. The more you work at building and developing your dropshipping business, the more you'll understand the concepts that are being presented. And while you are bound to make mistakes as you create your first dropshipping company, you should be aware that some mistakes are more costly than others. You never want to make a mistake on purpose and you should be willing to learn not only from your own missteps, but from the mistakes of others. In this chapter we'll go over common dropshipping pitfalls to watch out for.

Lack of Preparation

You may be eager to get started with dropshipping which is a good thing. But you don't want to let that excitement push you into overlooking important details in your business. Forgetting to set up a strong inventory management system, or neglecting to find a back-up supplier means that you are ill-prepared for the future. While it is possible to avoid disaster in the short-term through luck, you'll find that eventually your luck will run out. You must be prepared to deal with all manner of disasters in the dropshpping industry. Throughout this book we have talked a lot about the potential problems that will come your way. Anticipate them and create contingency plans to handle them. There are no prizes for getting caught unprepared in this business.

Becoming too dependent upon a supplier

Suppliers are extremely vital for your success as a dropshipper. Without them, you won't be able to sell your products online. However, this realization may create an unhealthy relationship with the supplier. The fear that you may end up losing their business and thus have to accept their bad business practices can be paralyzing. Some dropshippers end up solely trusting and focusing on a single supplier only to end up dealing with too many frustrations.

A supplier is nothing more than a means to an end. Sure, you want to have a good business relationship with them, but at the end of the day, you're working with professionals for the purpose of making money. They can and should be replaced if their actions or policies are affecting your bottom line negatively. You should be willing to look for new suppliers, especially as you grow your business. Remember, a supplier wants its products to sell because that is how they make money. If you come in with a proven track record, most will be happy to work with you. Some may even give you better deals than who you are currently working with.

Just don't fall into the trap of thinking that you need a single supplier in order to succeed. It creates an unhealthy dependence and can prevent you from accomplishing your goals in the future.

Neglecting to brand

Some dropshippers make the mistake of neglecting to create a strong brand for their company. They think that since their products aren't actually theirs, they have no reason to invest in creating a visual brand. After all, you can't just slap your logo onto the products you are selling, right? While that may be true, that doesn't mean that people visiting your site are looking for generic products. Rather, they are looking for a well designed website that fits the product identity that they are looking for. If you sell sports products, you'll want to form your company's brand identity around ideas that appeal to the sports fan. Pick bright colors in the design, use sporty models for your products and even have a graphic design that matches the theme and feel of a sports team, without violating any copyrights of course.

Branding is a shorthand in marketing. It is meant to evoke a certain kind of emotional and association. The goal is to get customers who see your brand to quickly associate those feelings and emotions with your products. A good brand will aid you greatly when it comes to marketing. But if you leave your website looking bare, with just a handful of products to buy and maybe a banner, you won't be evoking any kind of emotional response – except boredom! You cannot neglect branding just because you aren't directly involved in the creation of these products.

Slow Customer Service

When you're just starting out, your relationship with customers is extremely new and fragile. While there are many things for a business owner to handle in the world of dropshipping, communications from the customer are among the most important. Answering questions and replying to emails promptly is necessary if you are going to earn the trust of the customer. It can be easy to forget about sending an email, especially if you have a lot going on, so make sure that you prioritize any time that you receive an email from a customer. There's nothing worse than ignoring a customer's email for five or six days, especially if your reply would have helped motivate them to click on the buy button!

Wanting to see results right away

While the modern world is bent towards instant gratification, you should know that starting a business takes time. You won't see the fruit for quite a while. Those who want to see results right away may begin to panic as the weeks or months go by without a profit. This can lead to discouragement or simply giving up. The truth is that you won't make money instantly, in fact, you may end up simply losing money the first few time you try this out. This news isn't meant to discourage you, rather to give you a realistic view of what you are facing.

Building a business up is like planting a tree. There are a lot of things that go into the start, such as finding the right soil, figuring out when to plant the tree, etc, but at the end of the day, the only thing that will help a business or a tree grow is time. You will need to nurture and take care of your business, and the only way to do that is be patient with the end result. Eventually the money will start coming in, it just takes time.

Taking Ethical Shortcuts

Sometimes there are opportunities in the world of online business to bypass ethics in order to make a dollar. False claims, outright lies or swindling customers can be tempting when you consider how much money there is to make. Taking these shortcuts may make you money in the short term, but they will cause serious damage to your company and even to your personal reputation. The last thing that you need is to end up blacklisted from a serious merchant such as PayPal, only because you had a momentary lapse of ethics.

Wasting money on bold claims

There are some people out there who make all sorts of promises. "If you buy my product or course" they may say, "you'll learn everything you need to make a million in your first year!" While it is very possible to make a million dollars online, the chances of achieving that goal in the first year with dropshipping is incredibly slim. But there are many hucksters out there who are interested in selling you products, services and courses that do nothing other than making your wallet lighter.

107

Don't look to people who exhibit a get rich quick mentality. These folks do make their money, but they make it off of selling courses and books. Rather, look to proven professionals who are honest about the risk and difficulties of making money through dropshipping. Education is necessary, but you must pay close attention to the people who are trying to educate you. If they are offering ideas like "easy money" or "make a fortune while you sleep," you might do better to ignore them and look for more moderate claims.

This isn't to say that all courses and books are a waste of money. There are people out there who have worked hard, made a killing in their field and in the processed learned the ins and outs of the business. These people have a right to sell their information and experiences to you for money, but just make sure that they have actual, verifiable results to the claims that they are making.

Laziness

The biggest pitfall when it comes to not just the dropshipping industry, but any business endeavor is laziness. Oftentimes, we find ourselves pushing really hard at the beginning, but slowing down as the months go by. Usually, this is because the excitement of doing something new and interesting begins to fade away. Instead, we find ourselves struggling to maintain our workloads and worse yet, we might even begin to slack off.

Beginnings are always marked by excitement. There is a lot of new energy and passion that pushes us to get a lot of work done, but we can't stay in that honeymoon phase forever. Over time, those passions dwindle down and some people believe that loss of fever as a bad thing. Truth be told, losing that passion is to be expected. A lot of business practices are rather mundane, and sitting at your computer, sifting through the large amounts of data, figuring out what is trending or not can be rather boring.

This is usually the point where most casual people will begin to slink off. Without that excitement and energy, there is little reason to keep going. Those who don't quit may end up losing their focus and may start doing the bare minimum, simply maintaining their business instead of working to expand it. This kind of laziness is the product of missing the entire point of running a dropshipping operation. The point of any online business isn't to derive enjoyment from it 24/7. The point isn't to feel excited or happy about what you're doing. The point is to make money and lots of it.

Granted, excitement and happiness may come and go as you work. You may find satisfaction in the work, but at the end of the day, you're running a business because you want wealth and the freedoms that come with it. You may not find it to be a rewarding experience in the moment, but as you build your business up, you will know it's worth it. Don't let laziness ruin your chances at the big leagues. The fire will go out at some point, but discipline and hard work will make up for that fact in spades. And soon, you will find that something stronger and better replaces that fire: satisfaction in looking at what success you have achieved.

Chapter 14: Growing Your Dropshipping Business

Once you've created your dropshipping company, you'll want to begin focusing on developing a growth strategy. But before you can develop that strategy, you need to understand what the metrics are that we use to determine what growth looks like for a dropshipping company.

Metrics

Metrics are what allow us to measure effectiveness of our company. As a dropshipper, there are several key metrics that you want to pay attention to, these are:

1. Customer Acquisition

Customer acquisition is how many new customers are making first time purchases. You'll need to understand not only how to acquire customers, but also how much it costs in terms of advertising to gain a new customer. This cost is known as the Customer Acquisition Cost, or CAC for short.

2. Customer Retention

Once you've acquired new customers, you'll want to measure how many of these customers come back and make more purchases. Customer retention can often be neglected by those who are starting out with eCommerce. Rather, they follow the big dazzling idea of getting new customers, not realizing that 10 customers who buy 10 times is just the same as getting 100 first time buyers. A good dropshipper is able to create a relationship with customers that boost their retention number and ensures a steady flow of sales.

3. Website Traffic

Traffic to your website will help you get an idea of how many people are coming across your brand. While traffic can be valuable, it is important not to fixate on it as a measure of success. A million page hits does not equal a million sales. It is far better to figure out ways to generate high quality traffic that will buy your product rather than try to get as many people to visit you as possible.

4. Conversion Rates

A conversion is when a customer converts to a behavior that you want. In the case of dropshipping, a conversion means a sale. Conversion rates are calculated by the number of people who interact with your ads, or sales pages and then make a purchase. As you can guess, we want our conversion rates to be as high as possible.

There are plenty of other metrics to pay attention to as you grow your business, but the above four are the most integral to getting started with building a growth strategy. Here are seven powerful strategies that you can use to grow your business.

1: Use SEO

Search Engine Optimization, or SEO is the practice of making your website easy to find through web searches. As we discussed when talking about niches, customers discover websites through typing in keywords in search engines. By using those keywords in your product descriptions and throughout your site, you can help increase your ranking in the search engine. So if you organically talk about water bottles throughout your website, and someone types in water bottles on Google, you will show up somewhere on the rankings.

SEO will help create organic traffic for your company. You don't have to spend money on targeted advertising, rather, you just need to focus on identifying the right keywords that people in your niche are searching for. Once you've identified those keywords, you can sprinkle them throughout your website, putting them in product descriptions organically. Then, as people visit your website, the ranking will increase and soon, you may end up being one of the top results.

SEO is a serious business practice and make no mistake, you need to do it right if you want your business to get free traffic. The particulars of the practice, however, are outside of the scope of this book. We're mentioning it as number one on the list because it is seriously important for you to learn how it works. Spend your time learning how to do SEO properly, you won't regret it!

2: Create Attractive First Time Offers

You'll want to entice your customers into purchasing your goods. However, there is quite a barrier between you and prospective buyers, and that barrier is trust. When shopping online, there are plenty of things that can go wrong. Customers tend to be wary and discerning. To get them to move out of their comfort zone, the products must be interesting enough for them to make the decision to purchase it.

In order to help create the necessary motivation to make the first purchase, you should work to create some kind of attractive first-time offer. Whether it is a coupon code, free shipping or an item that you throw in with the product, you should use language that excites and interests them. Help them see that they are getting a great deal, just for making the first purchase. This will often generate more conversions.

3: **Write Good Copy**

Products need descriptions. While you may be tempted to just write a quick, effortless description of each product, you must realize that customers don't just glance at those words. They review them, study them for meaning and then make decisions about the products. Visuals are important, but good copy is a necessity if you want to persuade people to purchase your products.

Writing good copy isn't terribly hard to do. Simply give a thorough description of the product, extol its virtues and try to display how the product will solve the customer's needs. Not every product needs several paragraphs in order to get the idea across, but you should spend time customizing what you say about each product. Not only will this make your products look more attractive, but it will also help set you apart from the competition.

If you worry that you aren't a skilled writer, then you may want to consider hiring someone to write the copy for you. If you take that road, make sure that the individual that you hire is skilled with SEO as well as writing. By combining those two practices together, you will be greatly increasing your marketing efficiency.

4: Use Paid Marketing

Organic traffic is wonderful, but it can only go so far. If you want to increase your company's growth, then you are going to need to market. The only way to effectively market to your target audience is to use targeted marketing systems, such as Google Adwords or Facebook Ads. You may balk at the idea and instead try to grow your company with free methods, such as social media to talk about your products, but the fact of the matter is that you have to spend money to make money.

The good news is that regardless of your budget, you can market. Facebook only requires a minimum of $5 to get started, and offers highly targeted marketing, which means you will be putting ads for your products right in front of potential customer's faces. This has the highest chance of bringing you paid customers, and as you make money, you can invest more in your advertising budget, which in turns brings in more consumers.

Don't be afraid to spend money on paid marketing. It will bring in a higher quality of website traffic and can increase your chances of not only customer acquisition, but also customer retention. Thanks to retargeting systems, you can often track who has visited your site and as such, put ads in front of them to remind them that your product exists.

Paid marketing is extremely powerful and the data you can extrapolate from these efforts will aid you greatly in growing your business and refining your sales pitches. Take some time to study up on how to use paid marketing effectively and then set aside a monthly budget solely for advertising. Over time, you will see your efforts grow.

5: Collect Customer Emails

One of the best ways to retain customers is to have a method of collecting customer emails at the end of the shopping process. Usually, this is simple as having a checkbox that asks if they would like to get deals and discount codes emailed to them. Once you have collected an email, you can then send them newsletters and deals as often as you like. This free marketing tool is perfect, since you already have a track record with the customer. They've already bought your product once, as long as they enjoyed the experience and you treat their email with respect, you can increase the chances of them buying from you again and again.

6: Build a rating system

A rating system is one of the most invaluable ways to grow your business. When customers scour across your website, looking at products, they will be looking for reviews as well. Multiple five star reviews will indicate that not only is the product valuable, but that you, the company, are trustworthy. Adding a rating system to your products isn't difficult, in fact, some platforms might already have an automatic review system.

As long as you have good products and give a good customer experience, you don't have to worry about negative ratings. However, just because a customer is satisfied doesn't mean that they will automatically go online and rate your product. In fact, the majority of customers won't bother to rate a product at all, even if they love it. This can be a little frustrating, as you the retailer are dependent on good ratings.

So, one of your challenges, as you make sales, is to figure out an effective way to motivate your customers into reviewing your products. Customers who have bad experiences don't need much motivation, spite, frustration and anger tend to move them to click on the one star button. But a customer who has a good experience is less focused on displaying it to the world.

Therefore, it is pivotal that you remind your customer base that ratings are extremely important to your business. By sending out emails asking for reviews, or even including slips in your packaging that requests that a customer reviews the product, you increase your chances of getting a good review. Some customers don't even think about the idea of a review, so by reminding them, you may be motivating them to help you out.

While reviews are important, you should never compromise your integrity in order to gain them. Offering things like incentives, free products or even paying people to review your products is unethical. People should give reviews out of the joy they received from your product, not because you dangled a carrot in front of their faces. The worst case scenario is that customers who don't like the offer may end up posting a review of their own, informing everyone else of your attempts. This can torpedo any good reviews that you have on the rest of your site, as most people will then assume you've bought all the reviews on the website.

7: Use Social Media

Social media is extremely important to your business endeavors. While paid marketing is the best way to acquire new customers, social media marketing allows for you to maintain relationships with your fanbase. It will allow for you to have conversations with customers, answer questions and even share pictures of people who are enjoying your product. You will want to have a strong social media hub, utilizing platforms such as Facebook or Instagram, just so that people who like your product can follow you.

Social media provides more than just simple presence, it also gives you the ability to see what the passions and interests of your followers are. By engaging and interacting with them, you can get a sense of who your customer is. In the process, this can help you fine tune your inventory and give you new ideas for products to sell.

Of course, you should be cautious when utilizing social media. Yes, you will want to grow your business and your brand, but you also don't want to risk spending too much time promoting yourself. Leave that to paid advertising. If people only see you talking about your own products and yourself, they'll end up coming to the conclusion that your brand doesn't care about others and you're a bit of a shill. However, if you take an interest in what other people are saying, share dialogue and contribute value to others, you will be able to foster a deeper connection with followers. In turn, this builds trust and the few times that you do mention your products, your followers will have a better chance of listening to what you have to say.

Chapter 15: Tips and Tricks for Success

This chapter is a collection of different tips and tricks that many successful dropshippers have used in their quest to make money online. These ideas will hopefully get you thinking of the many different ways that you can improve your business as you go along.

Find Products That You Love

Passion is hard to contain. If you find that you're struggling with caring about certain niches, then you might want to consider looking areas that you are personally passionate about. The more you love and care about a product, the more motivated you will be to sell it to others. Not only that, but you'll also have a keen insight in how to market the product properly, as you will have inside knowledge about the products.

Don't Chase Trends

There is a big difference between finding what is beginning to move upwards in a trend, and what trends have already peaked. The best place to be with a trend is at the beginning, as it begins to rapidly rise upwards. However, many dropshippers end up doing the opposite. They see a field that has already peaked and jump in, hoping to make money off of some brand new trend. This often ends in disaster, as the market has already been saturated with entrepreneurs who all had the same idea and ultimately the bubble pops.

The best time to be a part of a fad is before people realize it's a fad. Trying to move rapidly into a new space is risky and might be a waste of time and resources. The real trick is learning how to determine whether or not a trend has already peaked or not. In general, try to pay attention to what the market and the tastemakers are saying. The moment someone can identify the next "big" is the moment the bubble will begin to swell. Remember, the people who made the most money during the Gold Rush were the folks selling shovels, not the gold diggers.

Automate As Much as You Can

While there is value in learning how to dropship manually, the truth is that automation is the best way to increase your business size and structure. More automation means that you are able to scale faster, without getting tangled up in a lot of busy work. Automation also means that there will be fewer operator mistakes. You don't want to get in the way of your own business, so look for as many automation options as possible as you build your dropshipping website. Yes, there will be costs to using these services, but these costs are well worth it, especially as you begin to scale upwards.

Once you are making decent money, you might want to consider hiring a virtual assistant to fill in the gaps for tasks that require human intelligence. By hiring a virtual assistant who is familiar with dropshipping, you can shave off hours of important tasks, such as market research or customer service. The best part is that a virtual assistant doesn't need to work in house, rather they can be located anywhere in the world. As long as they are familiar with the business process, they can assist you with the tasks that a machine simply cannot do.

Another form of automation is the creation of chatbots for your website. A chatbot is an artificial intelligence that is able to communicate with potential customers, answer questions and when they receive too difficult of a question, can simply refer the customer over to you. Chatbots help cut down on common customer service questions. Asking about availability, shipping rates or other types of information via email can take too long and frankly, can be automated. The fact that a customer can get information right away also improves their experience greatly.

Run More Dropshipping Sites

Once you begin to grow, you may see that there is potential for increasing your dropshipping revenue by selling other types of products. However, since you are running a niche site, you may realize that certain products don't fit in with your brand. Rather than try to dilute your brand by including products that simply don't belong, you should create a new website and a new brand.

Since you already have suppliers and a fairly successful dropshpping site, replicating that success shouldn't be difficult. The only real risk you are taking is in the new niche you are targeting. But, if that niche succeeds, you have essentially doubled your profit potential!

Running multiple dropshipping sites isn't easy, however and shouldn't be done until you feel that you have a firm handle on your first site. Once you've made enough money and feel comfortable with what you're doing, then you should scale. But if you're still struggling to make a profit, don't try to add to your stress by opening a second operation. However, with that being said...

Don't be afraid to kill your niche

If you picked a niche that simply isn't performing well, you might be tempted to hold on and see if things improve. While there is something to be said about patience, there is also something to be said about learning when to fold your cards. Some niches simply don't take off or have enough customers to justify all of the effort of dropshipping. If that's the case, you would do better to simply revamp your website and focus on another niche.

The speculative nature of finding niches means that this might happen a few times. Don't be discouraged. Finding that special area with low competition and high amounts of customers is incredibly hard to do, but once you finally get it, you'll have an established revenue stream for a long time to come. What you can't risk is getting too stuck on a niche that simply isn't working.

So how long should you wait to see a profit from your efforts? It depends, but in general, if all of your marketing efforts barely return anything and you've spent a good six months working to build the business up as much as possible, it's time to call it quits and move on.

One danger that can be present in making these decisions is known as the Sunk Cost Fallacy. It goes something like this. "I've invested six months already, if I give up now, then I will have lost all of that time and money. Therefore, I must keep going in order for it all to be worth it." This is also known as Gambler's Logic, the idea that just because you lost X amount of resources means that walking away is the bad decision. The truth is, if you keep going, you will only be losing more of your time and money, just like if a gambler keeps losing money, but stays at the table, he will still lose more.

There is a time to be patient with your investment, but you should learn how to discern between patience and holding on for too long. Don't let the sunk cost fallacy get a grip on you. Chances are if a niche isn't paying off in six months, it won't pay off in month seven, eight or nine. Back up the website, and move on to trying another niche.

Keep an eye on the competition

You will have competitors in the field that you are selling in. It is important for you to keep an eye on them. Try to identify the top five competitors in your field and make a point to visit their websites every so often. Look at how they are presenting their products, what kind of sales they are offering and what their prices are.

The last thing you want is for a competitor to be undercutting you on price, especially if you are unaware of it. By keeping an eye on the competition, you'll be able to ensure that your prices are competitive and that no one is cleverly sniping customers from under your nose. Better yet, you may find areas that your competitors are weak in and come up with ways to push past them.

Integrate Social Media

Social media integration is important if you want to create what is known as social proof. Social proof is the idea that if you can real people to talk about and show off their products, others will look at that as a form of proof that the products are good. We live in an era of tremendous social proof, with thousands upon thousands looking at recommendations from their Instagram feeds and on Twitter.

If you want to generate more sales through word of mouth marketing, then you should create ways to integrate social media into your website. Whether it's a simple share button, or the ability for the customer to tell others that they just bought X product, you need to have accessibility so people can quickly share their experiences with others. Even a single share can be shown to hundreds of people, which may increase the chances of someone clicking onto your website and buying a few products!

Pay Attention to Seasons

Seasonal shopping, especially around the holidays can be huge. Regardless of what type of product you're selling, you should try to look into finding out if there is some way that you can capitalize on the upcoming holiday seasons. Christmas is one of the most important consumer holidays out there and if you can find ways to capitalize on it with your niche, you will have a very profitable fourth quarter.

Likewise, some products and niches can actually suffer due to seasonal interests. You should make sure that whatever products you are dropshipping can either sell all year round, or that you have another niche that you focus on during the off-season.

Sometimes you won't be sure how a niche will perform during a season. If that's the case, make sure you closely monitor the situation and measure how well things are going. If you find that a niche suffers intensely during a certain holiday season, but does well throughout the rest of the year, you should keep that in mind for the future. Don't make the mistake of thinking that these situations are anomalies. Most online shopping is cyclical, so take a note and prepare for what is to come next time.

Pay attention to the news

The online world is constantly buzzing and humming with new changes. Between government shifts in online policy, trends that come in and out of style and changes in the way social media works, a lot can happen in just a month. If you stay out of the loop, certain policies or trends could shift on you, moving the market away from you and leaving you stranded. Don't make the mistake of assuming that things stay the same forever with online commerce. That's simply not the case. You need to be like a shark, swimming constantly, on the lookout for new opportunity and new threats. If you don't pay attention to online news regarding your chosen niches and e-commerce in general, you could potentially miss out on a lot! So make a point to never stop reading the news.

Learn from analytics

One of the biggest advantages behind using online businesses is the fact that data is easy to collect. Whether it's from Facebook advertising or website traffic, you can sit down and look at the type of customer that is interacting with your products.

This can provide you with powerful insights into what age group your product resonates with, where your major sources of traffic are coming from and how effective your marketing practices have been.

If you want to be good at dropshipping, you'll have to master learning how to analyze and interpret analytics. Accessing this data is easy enough, by using Google Analytics to monitor your web traffic, you can create comprehensive pictures of the type of person you are interacting with. Not only that, but you can also create specific events through Google Analytics, such as link clicks. This will give you the ability to see how many people are clicking on specific links throughout your website.

This gives you the power to tell how people are interacting with your site, which products are most popular, how long people stay on each page, etc. Mastering a deep understanding of these analytics will allow for you to modify your website on the fly, eliminating pages or products that aren't gaining a following. Really, if you want to be great at dropshipping, you'll want to learn how to process and interpret data that you have collected.

Chapter 16: Promoting Your Dropshipping Business

Building up a company from scratch requires a significant amount of promotion. We've already discussed paid, targeting advertising as one of the primary ways that you can promote your business, but that's not the only way.

Promoting your company is really promoting your brand. People aren't interested in companies, they are interested in brands and the identities that they represent. Customers are looking for brands that they have similarities to, brands that celebrate their interests and passions. Therefore, if you want to promote your company, you'll need to promote the brand first and foremost.

What does this require? First, you need a clear brand identity, which we have already discussed. Brand identity is a combination of visual design and message. What is your company about? What problems are you solving? What is your company's passion? By answering these questions, you can create a strong message that will hopefully resound with your target demographic.

Once you've figured out what your message is, it's then your job to spread that message to the rest of the world. This is really what promotion is. It is sharing the solutions to the problems that your niche deals with. This is an important mindset to have. Your product will help them, and that is your message to them. It's not about making you rich, it's about providing value to others. As long as you hold to those principles, you will be able to authentically promote your business.

The promotion process of a business is what's known as a sales funnel. In order to better understand marketing, you have to understand the steps that a customer goes through before they make a purchase.

Step One: Awareness

Before a customer can purchase a product, they must become aware of the product. Generating awareness in a customer is one of your first major challenges as a marketer. There are many different ways to go about generating awareness, but the most important thing to remember is that your goal is to help the customer become aware of the solution to their problem.

Once a customer has entered into the awareness phase, they will either interact with your company and begin to explore, or they may simply ignore your promotional efforts. Those who begin to interact are moved down the funnel, into the Interest phase.

Step Two: Interest

The interesting phase is where the potential customer begins to interact with your product. They begin to explore, ask questions about the product and generally learn more. For example, if someone sees an ad that you are running and begins to poke around on your website, observing the few products that you have, they are taking an active interest in your product. This opens up the potential to them making a purchase.

Moving a customer from the awareness phase to the interest phase can be difficult. Getting someone to see your ad isn't nearly as hard as getting them to click on it. In general, you will want to work to create intriguing advertisements or promotions that highlight the value that your product is bringing to people's lives.

Once the customer has spent enough time in the interest phase, they will automatically move on to the next step in the sales funnel, the decision stage.

Step Three: Decision

The decision point happens when the customer chooses how they want to interact with your product. They have three options, they can say "yes," and buy the product, "no" and click away from your site or "maybe later" in which they will leave and consider their options. Perhaps they will spend more time in the interest phase, at which point they will ultimately come to a yes or no decision.

After they have carefully evaluated the facts and data that you have provided them, they will either commit to purchasing or leave. This is what it is important for you to do everything in your power to ensure that your customers have all the pertinent information about your product. A lack of information often leads customers to decide against making the purchase, or worse, moving towards another competitor who has better information than you.

But supposing that the customer makes the choice to purchase, they move into the penultimate stage, the action stage.

Step Four: Action

The action step is a positive step for the customer. This is where they begin to go about the task of actually making the purchase. Normally, this should be a painless process. Be warned that you must work to make the checkout phase as smooth and quick as possible. If you fail to create an obstacle free pathway, the customer may end up having second thoughts and abandoning their cart. So make sure that you do everything in your power to have a quick and effortless checkout phase.

Once the customer has made the purchase, they have successfully passed through the funnel! These four steps might seem simple, but you should spend time working on each part. Look at each step of the funnel and ask yourself, what would be the best way to move a customer onto the next step?

Your message is an important part of the sales funnel, as it is going to be one of the primary ways that you capture the attention of potential customers. Below is a list of different ideas and concepts that you can use to help move leads through the sales funnel in a healthy, organic manner.

Run a Giveaway

Giveaways are a great way to do two things, first to generate an email list of potential leads, and secondly, to make people aware of your product. The idea of free can be a powerful motivator and if a potential customer sees that you are giving away a product that appeals to them, they will be tempted to sign up for the promotion. Even if they lose the contest, they still have an awareness of your product. Better yet, if they are disappointed at this loss, they very well may end up visiting your site later on and still buying the product!

Giveaways help generate product awareness. When you're brand new on the scene, a good giveaway can make all the difference in the world. Best of all, they can be fairly cheap to run, as the biggest costs that you will incur is acquiring the product, which is at a wholesale price anyway.

Running a giveaway is fairly easy to do, all you need is to use a program, such as Gleam.io, which will help run the contest automatically. All you need to do is put in the perimeters of the contest, what type of actions customers will need to take to get entry into the contest and then the time the contest is being run. After that, it's just a matter of distributing news about this contest, which is mostly done through social media and email campaigns.

One mistake to steer clear of is giving away a product that is too attractive. You don't want to get people outside of your niche entering the contest, or else they will just take the free product and leave. Instead, focus on giving away a niche product that attracts the exact customer that you want browsing your site later on. This will greatly increase your chances of getting a sale.

Run a Blog

If you want to sell products, you'll need to generate traffic on your website. One of the best ways to passive generate that traffic is to give people a reason to visit, even if they aren't interested in making purchases. You can do this through running a blog on your business site.

A blog that has relevant and useful information for your target niche will generate passive traffic. As they visit your blog, they'll have repeated exposure to your products as well as casual mentions of sales and deals that you have going on. If the blog is high quality and provides good content, you may end up establishing yourself as an authority on your niche. This will greatly improve your rankings when it comes to Search Engine Optimization. Not only that, it may attract customers from similar niche websites to follow you instead.

You may not be a writer or may not feel that you have enough time to run a blog. If that's the case, then it may be prudent to hire a freelancer who will be able to create enough content for your website in exchange for a fee. Usually these professional are skilled enough to create engaging and useful content for your customer, so it can be worth the investment. However, before you spend too much on hiring a writer, you should at least be making some level of money off of your website. You want to use the blog to facilitate growth, not as a strict marketing move.

Sponsorship

One great way to promote your brand while also giving back to the niche community is to financially sponsor a content creator who is in your targeted niche. For example, you could sponsor a podcast, paying them a specific fee and in exchange, they'll run advertisements on their platform. This can be a huge way to promote your brand while also tapping into an already established market.

The benefits can be extremely targeted marketing. While certain types of ads, like Facebook or Google Adwords have lower levels of conversion rates, sponsoring a podcast can be significantly higher. This is because podcast listeners trust the podcast host that they tune into weekly. If the host is willing to talk or promote a product, it's because he genuinely approves of the product, especially if it is pertinent to his niche.

It's important to note that sponsorship is different from paid reviews. A podcast or YouTube host must disclose that they have a sponsorship and you cannot dictate how they talk about your product, or else you start to veer into unethical territory. But there is nothing wrong with sponsoring a popular voice within your niche community and receiving promotion because of it. Even if the content creator isn't kind to your product, you can at least get valuable feedback about ways to improve. Of course, it is rare to have a content creator bite the hand that feeds. If you have a good product, then you have nothing to worry about.

Create Product Reviews

While paying a customer to review a product can be considered unethical, there are ways that you can facilitate the creation of product reviews. One such way would be to contacting content creators who review products in your niche and offering to send them a review copy for free. This is a common practice in the industry and most product reviewers will disclose that they received a free copy.

If the content creator accepts, you can send the product to them and hope for a positive review. If your product is up to snuff and the creator likes it, you have a multiplication effect. First, the creator's audience will automatically gain awareness of your product. By offering something like a special discount code to the audience, you can increase your chances of conversion even higher.

Second, you now have content that you can directly link on your website. Since a third party is the one doing the review, it will create a stronger level of social proof about the value of your product. A person who is browsing around on your website, may click on the video and end up watching the entire review. This can be an effective way to increase sales, and the content creator will appreciate the opportunity to have more viewers.

Another type of product review is what's known as a demonstration. Rather than have an independent party review the value of the product, you create a video demonstration that shows the product in action. This can be invaluable for customers who are still looking for reasons to be convinced to buy your product. A quick video, showing the ins and outs of the product, giving clear examples of its use can go a long way.

Create Affiliate Opportunities

Affiliate marketing is one of the big ways of making money online, with individuals working hard creating niche sites that review and refer people to good products. An affiliate marketer talks about the product, extols the virtues and provides what's known as an affiliate link. If a customer clicks on the affiliate link and makes a purchase, the marketer is paid a commission.

This is one of the oldest and most effective ways of marketing. But as a dropshipper, your role won't be as the affiliate marketer, but rather the product publisher who is offering the commission. By offering commissions to affiliate marketers, they will go out and do all the hard work, promoting your product, referring people and generating awareness. In exchange, you pay them a piece of the profits.

Working with affiliate marketers can be a great way to generate sales for your product without much effort on your part. The only downside is that you will have to pay a mission to the people who are bringing in those customers. Still, as the age old question goes, what's 100% of nothing? It's better to have 80% profit of 100 sales than it is to have no sales.

Putting together an affiliate program isn't hard, you just need to create terms of service, make affiliate links, design some banners and go out searching for bloggers and influencers who are in your niche. Contact them and tell them and see if they are interested in an affiliate deal. Most of these people are already used to affiliate marketing and are looking for more opportunities. Having higher than standard commission rates can work wonders when it comes to attracting new affiliate marketers to work with.

Create a Lead Magnet

If you've captured the interest of an individual who is part of your target market, but they haven't moved onto the purchase action yet, you would consider that person to be a lead. They have the potential to convert, but they just aren't ready yet. One of the problems with the internet is that since there is so much to do, people can often click away from your website and completely forget that it exists. Worse yet, they may have actually liked your product,t but an email or hilarious picture of a cat distracted them long enough to forget.

A lead magnet is what will help you capture the email of potential leads. Then, later on, you'll be able to send emails to the lead, offering deals and discounts. Thus, if the lead was in the decision or interest phase, you can motivate them to finalize and make a purchase.

Getting an email from a non-customer can be difficult, which is why we create incentives known as lead magnets. These incentives are targeted specifically to your niche customer and are offered free, in exchange for an email. For example, if you are running a fishing niche site, a potential lead magnet might be a free eBook on the best techniques for fly fishing. If this catches the interest of the lead, they'll sign up, giving you access to their email in exchange for this book.

Lead magnets are powerful ways to promote your products. Once you have a lead's email, you can send them offers directly to their inbox. This captures the direct attention of the customer and as long as the offer in your email is attractive, you run a higher chance of a conversion from them. Best of all, if the customer simply forgot to make the purchase, or was delaying due to a number of reasons, the email serves as a helpful reminder that you still exist.

Creating a lead magnet shouldn't be too difficult. You want to make sure that you avoid making the magnet too attractive, or else you will have low quality leads sign up. If the magnet is too broad, you may end up getting leads that will never convert. Instead, try to create a magnet that would only appeal to your target market and is easy to make.

The two most basic types of lead magnets are either eBooks or discount codes. Free shipping, 50 percent off or two for one deals can be a big enough motivator to convince a lead to hand over their email. Or, a free eBook with valuable information can be just as motivating. You'll want to make sure that either way, the lead is of good quality and does as it promises. The last thing you want is for a lead to sign up for your mailing list and end up getting a dud as reward. This can cause frustration and immediate distrust from the customer.

There are plenty of services out there that assist with the creation of eBooks, if that is the road you want to take. You don't have to be a brilliant writer or a graphic designer, you can outsource that and have a nice, short book that helps to solve a customer problem, all the while promoting your business.

Another thing to note is that when you get a customer's email, it's important to treat it with respect. Spamming them too many times will result in them unsubscribing. Finding leads is hard and expensive work, you don't want to undo it all by sending twenty emails a week.

Conclusion

The path to becoming a successful dropshipper isn't an easy one. It takes a lot of time, energy and effort, but if you are willing to walk down this road, you will find that there are tremendous rewards to be had. The freedom of being your own boss, the exhilaration of seeing your sales grow, week by week and the pleasure of getting a paycheck for all of those efforts are second to none.

Throughout this book, we've discussed the many ways that you can create, grow and thrive as a dropshipping specialist. The most important principle to hold to is that no matter what the endeavor is, no matter how much you read, there is simply no replacement for hustle and grit. The only thing left to do now is to create a business plan and get to work. Good luck out there!

Before we begin I have a free gift for you from Russell Brunson - for those of you that don't know Russell Brunson is, he's the man that created Click Funnels. In my opinion it's the best funnel website out there and it has also helped create the most millionaires. Any form of passive income you are going to build, you will 100% need to leverage funnels of some sort. If you're reading this book, then you want to be the best in your industry. This book will give you the play by play to have people PAYING you for your advice. I am able to give you his best selling book for free right down here. I only have a few copies left so please get them while you can. Just click this http://bit.ly/giftfunnelbook